What is an Icon?

Copyright © 1999 Talanton Press

Published by Talanton Press, PO Box 390360, Mountain View, CA 94039-0360 USA
Email *talanton@bigfoot.com*

ISBN: 1-930224-00-1 English Edition
ISBN: 1-930224-01-X Russian Edition
ISBN: 1-930224-02-8 Greek Edition

Что такое икона?

© 1999 Талантон Пресс

Издано Talanton Press, PO Box 390360, Mountain View, CA 94039-0360 USA
Email *talanton@bigfoot.com*

ISBN: 1-930224-00-1 на английском языке
ISBN: 1-930224-01-X на русском языке
ISBN: 1-930224-02-8 на греческом языке

Τί εἶναι ἡ εἰκόνα;
© 1999 Talanton Press

Talanton Press, P.O. Box 390360, Mountain View, CA 94039-0360 USA
Email: *talanton@bigfoot.com*

ISBN: 1-930224-00-1 Ἀγγλική ἔκδοση
ISBN: 1-930224-01-X Ρωσσική ἔκδοση
ISBN: 1-930224-02-8 Ἑλληνική ἔκδοση

What is an
Icon?

What is an icon?

Have you ever seen an icon?

An icon is a holy picture of our Lord Jesus Christ, the Theotokos, or a saint that we venerate.

When we venerate an icon, we show our love for the saint and ask the saint to pray for us.

How do we venerate an icon?

First, we bless ourselves
with the sign of the Cross:
In the Name of the Father and of
the Son and of the Holy Spirit. Amen.
Then we kiss the holy icon. We ask
the saint to pray to God for us or for
someone we love.

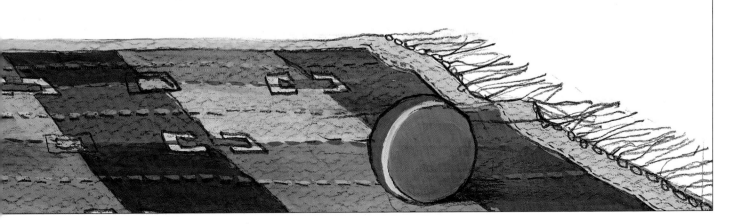

An icon can also show us something special that happened in the life of our Lord Jesus Christ or in the life of the Most Holy Theotokos.

One icon in the Church shows us the Nativity (birth) of our Lord Jesus Christ. Another icon shows the Lord on Palm Sunday as He went into Jerusalem riding on a donkey.

Another icon shows us the Lord's Resurrection — we venerate this icon on Holy Pascha.

Maria loves to go to church.

In the church there are many icons. Maria especially loves to venerate the icon of the Theotokos.

Maria also has many icons
in her house.

In her family icon corner,
where Maria says her
evening and morning prayers,
there are icons of our Lord Jesus Christ,
the Theotokos, Saint John the Baptist,
Saint Anna, and Saint Stephen.

In front of them burns an oil lamp.
Maria's daddy refills the oil lamp
when it burns low.

In the kitchen of Maria's home, there is an icon of Saint Euphrosynos the Cook. While Saint Euphrosynos was living in the monastery, he visited Paradise and picked three apples from a tree there. Can you see the apples in his hand?

In the dining room there is an icon of the Mystical Supper. The Lord Jesus Christ is eating with His disciples. Can you find Saint John the Theologian? He is leaning on the Lord's chest. The Lord loved Saint John very much.

In Maria's bedroom there is an icon of the Theotokos. She is holding the Lord Jesus Christ. Do you know why? One day the Archangel Gabriel came to her and said, "Rejoice! You will have a Baby, and you will name Him Jesus."

She answered, "I am ready to do whatever God wants me to do."

Maria shares her bedroom with her baby brother, Stephen. Above Stephen's crib hangs an icon of Saint Stephen, the First Martyr.

A martyr is someone who sheds his blood and gives his life for Christ.

Saint Stephen was also a deacon. He has a censer in his hand, just like the deacons in the church.

In Daddy and Mommy's bedroom there are two icons. Mommy's saint is Saint Anna, the mother of the Theotokos.

Daddy's saint is Saint John the Baptist, who told everybody that Christ would be coming soon.

When Saint John was a little baby, he was fed by an angel. After he grew up, he ate only wild sprouts and honey.

There is an icon in the car, too. It is an icon of the Theotokos. She protects everyone who prays to her.

Once she even protected a whole city from danger with her veil.

A special day for Maria is
Bright Monday — the day after Pascha.
All the children bring icons from
their homes to the church. After
the end of the Divine Liturgy,
the children follow in a
procession around
the church.

Do you have any special icons? Maybe you have an icon of your saint by your bed or in your family's prayer corner. You can ask your saint to pray for you.

Glory be to God for all the icons we can see and venerate!